THE SEVEN DEADLY SINS OF EXTERNAL TIMBER DESIGN

Revised 2014

EDGAR (TED) STUBBERSFIELD

About the Author

Ted Stubbersfield was born in the small Queensland town of Gatton in 1950. After studying to be a pastor in Brisbane and the UK he returned to the family business, Gatton Sawmilling Co. A fair question would be, can anything good come out of Gatton? Well, Gatton was the home of a Governor General of Australia (William Vanneck 1938). It is also the home of the best and most innovative hardwood producer in Australia, Outdoor Structures Australia (OSA).

The family had been involved in sawmilling and building for about 140 years and a lot of knowledge has passed through the generations. In 1985 we ventured into the footbridge market (almost by accident) and then followed public landscaping. Initially we just did as we were told by consultants who knew very little about timber. In about 1988 Ted decided he would come to know the medium he was working with far better than any of his competitors and most of the professionals who used his products.

Ted realised that there were no useful standards and guides for designing and building weather exposed timber structures such as boardwalks. That led in 1997 to his first formal research project on boardwalk design, engineering supply and construction. Over the years there followed a complete set of guides. These allowed professionals to design timber structures of exceptional beauty and durability. Typically, everybody wants to re-invent the wheel and the guides were usually ignored. Invariably, the same mistakes keep being made over and over. This little book is an attempt to remedy this.

In 2012, the time came to close the manufacturing arm of OSA and to take on a less stressful lifestyle. Ted plans to put in writing much of what he has learnt so the industry does not have to relearn it. This book is the third in a series of Timber Design Files that are intended to allow designers avoid the pitfalls of common but often bad practice and Standards that are very inadequate and engender a false sense of security.

List of Abbreviations

ACQ   Ammonia Copper Quaternary
CCA   Copper chrome arsenic
OSA   Outdoor Structures Australia

Note: Products formerly produced by OSA can now be purchased through the licensees to its IP. Contact the author for an updated list

Licensees are sought for southern and Western Australia and the USA

Contents

Introduction

When we talk of The Seven Deadly Sins what comes to mind? Is it wrath, greed, sloth, pride, lust, envy, and gluttony and old images such as Hieronymus Bosch's iconic painting "The Seven Deadly Sins". I suppose most of us have all committed our fair share of these over the years. (Perhaps some of my readers have committed more than their fair share). But don't worry; this is a book about external timber design, not theology.

Over the years I had been collecting what I thought were the worst mistakes in timber design and when I added them up there were seven. They appropriately came to be called "The Seven Deadly Sins of External Timber Design". The symmetry was spoilt when I added an eighth but you have to admit, it is a great title even if the count is now wrong.

While the more well known list of Seven Deadly Sins can be put down to the human condition, the same cannot be said when it comes to failures in timber design. As professionals it is important to master the medium in which you work. It is learnable and it is logical. What follows is an explanation of what these "sins" are and how to avoid them. Much of what you will read here has already been included in other guides but it is helpful to bring them all together in one spot and reinforce the points made.

Disclaimer

The information shown herein does not constitute a complete design so a Consulting Engineer with skills in both timber design and foundation systems should be engaged for the structural and foundation design.

Deadly Sin 1 – Not Having a Self Cleaning Deck

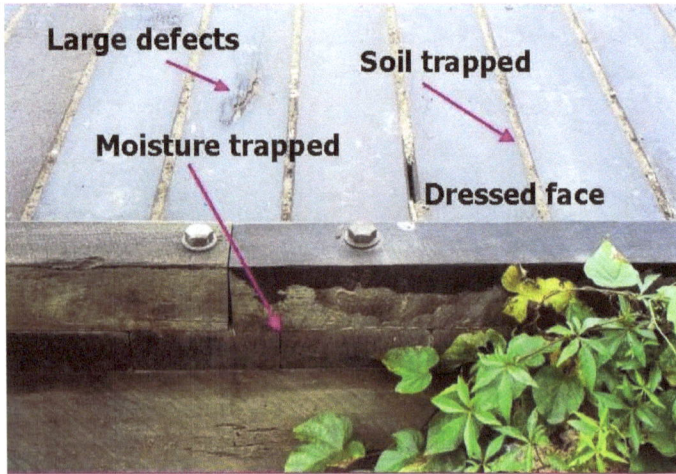

Figure 1. Poor detailing of deck and kerb

A highly respected authority on timber in the Australian setting, Colin MacKenzie, (Technical Director of Timber Queensland), has three requirements for a long lived timber structure – These are

- Keep them dry
- Don't let the rain get to them
- Don't let them get wet!

All three are hard to achieve with boardwalks and unroofed decks so the compromise is to detail the structure so it dries as soon as possible. The deck in Figure 1 shows a boardwalk deck that breaks this rule. The problems are:

- The kerb is coach-screwed straight onto the deck. This can reduce the life of the structure as:
  - ➢ The deck is not self cleaning. Any leaf litter is trapped on the deck. The build-up of moisture along the kerb can significantly reduce the life of the decking
  - ➢ Moisture is trapped between the kerb and the deck. Note that there is no gap between the boards under the kerb but a sizeable gap directly behind the kerb. Dry timber does not decay
- The decking has parallel sides with an arrised top. The gaps have filled with soil which will hold moisture.

My *Boardwalk Design Guide* has our recommendations on the detailing of kerbs and other edge treatments and gives timber sizes. Ideally, the kerbs need to be about 50 mm off the deck to be self cleaning and 75 mm for Australian disability requirements.

For details on designing a self cleaning deck refer to my *Boardwalk Design Guide.* The patented Deckwood^{tm} profile has the major advantage of being pre-graded and non reversible. The image above shows decking that was thicknessed (dressed) on the back but, being reversible, has been laid with some dressed faces up (i.e. the side that is slippery and has poorer weathering ability). The defects that should have gone down now present a splinter hazard to the public and will quickly deteriorate further.

Deadly Sin 2 – Not Designing Joists for Durability

Figure 2. Degrade of 50 mm joists

Careful attention must to be given to detailing the joist to ensure that after the decking has served its useful life, the substructure is still structurally sound and does not need to be replaced as well.

Heavy decking (35 mm plus), if face fixed, should be fastened with at least 14# (6mm) screws. As the joist seasons it invariably splits along the top face. Over the years moisture accumulates in the split and the timber eventually decays along the screw line as the image shows. When random length decking is used it must, by necessity, be joined on a joist. When this happens four screws are then forced into the top of the joist in close proximity causing severe damage to the joist and degrade is even more certain.

To maximise the life of the substructure we recommend:

- The use of a durable species such as OSA's Joistwood. Many Above Ground Durability 2 hardwoods give a short life, perhaps as little as 10-12 years
- Pre-oiling the joist with CN Oil
- Applying a liberal coat of CN Emulsion to where the joists touch the headstocks/bearer
- Installing the screws in a staggered alignment (run to a stringline), a minimum of 8 mm each side of the centreline
- That all Joists are a minimum of 75mm wide
  - As the screw should be four diameters i.e. 24 mm from the edge. A 50 mm joist does not allow for any staggering of the screws
- Ensuring the builder fully pre-drills to the full depth of the screw
  - "Batten screws" were designed to be used under a roof without pre-drilling so the natural reaction will be to use them in external structures in the same way
- Placing a layer of 110 mm malthoid dampcourse on top of the 75mm joists
  - Do not predrill 6mm through the dampcourse, use an undersize bit
- Designing for the join
  - Use set length decking
  - Join on a double joist with the screws at least 75mm from the end.

The above instructions have been described as a belt and braces approach, which is true. The cost and inconvenience of replacing more than just the decking is such that it demands that every step be taken to ensure there are no avoidable problems. Figures 2 and 4 show the effect on the joist of incorrect screw fastening. Correct fastening is shown in Figure 3, joining on a double joist is illustrated in Figure 5.

Our recommendations for detailing the joist for durability can be found in our *Deckwood Selection Guide*.

The decking was installed on the joist illustrated in Figure 3 following the instructions in our *Boardwalk Construction Guide* at the time (prior to the addition of malthoid). After **two years** there is still no splitting of the joist associated with the screw fixings. The use of malthoid dampcourse reinforces the effects of good practice.

Figure 3. Joist did not split as screws were installed correctly.

The image in Figure 4 was taken about **two months** after the completion of the boardwalk which is built on 75 mm joists as we recommend.

Unfortunately the screws shown in Figure 4 have not been staggered. As well, three screws are used when two were sufficient. The joist is badly split from one end to the other. Decay in the joist will be premature. We find that some do not like the aesthetics of the staggered alignment. If this is an insurmountable obstacle it is important that the joist should not be timber.

Figure 4. 75mm joist has split as screws are installed incorrectly.

Figure 5. Joining decking on a double joist

The ideal decking join detail is shown in Figure 5 which illustrates the advantages of using a double joist. The screws are a good distance from the end so there is no splitting of the decking. There is no damage to the joist by having too many fasteners. Note that the ends of the boards do not touch which ensures moisture is not held against the end grain by capillary action.

Deadly Sin 3 – Incorrect Use of Heart in Hardwood

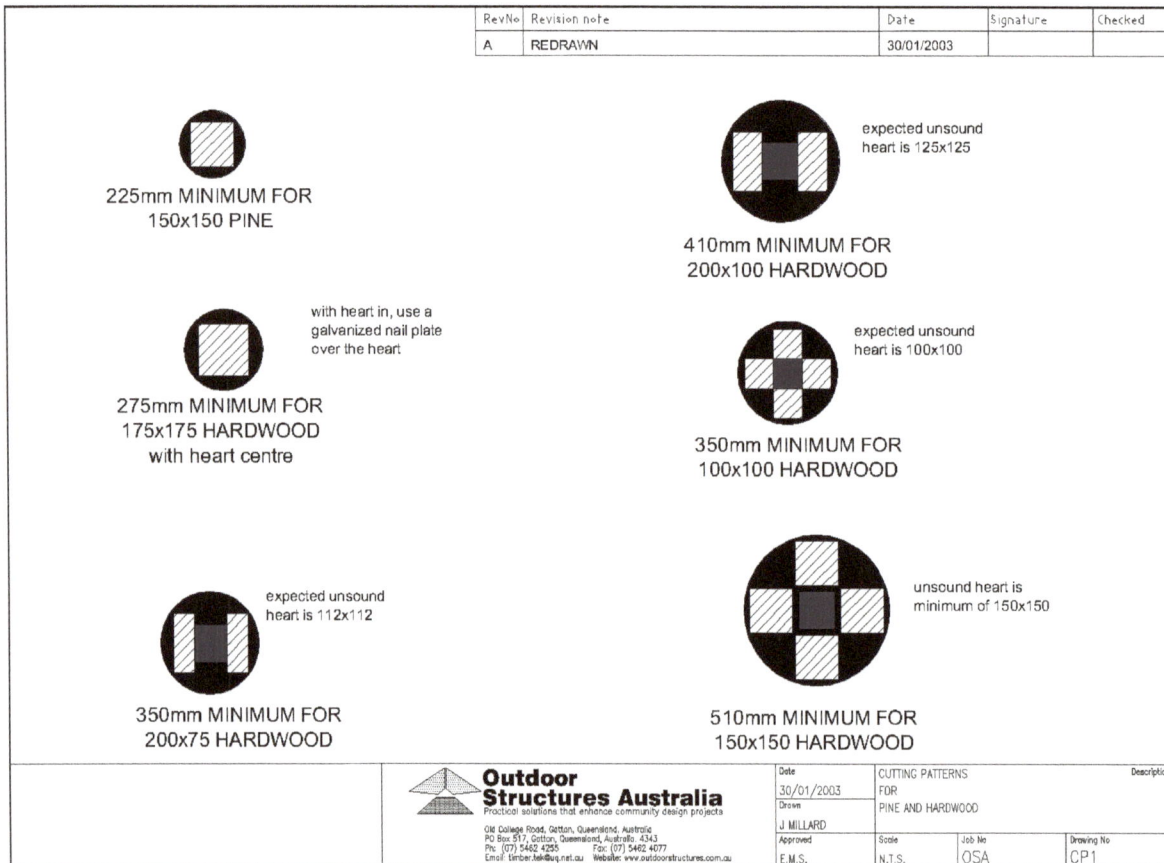

RevNo	Revision note	Date	Signature	Checked
A	REDRAWN	30/01/2003		

225mm MINIMUM FOR
150x150 PINE

expected unsound
heart is 125x125

410mm MINIMUM FOR
200x100 HARDWOOD

with heart in, use a
galvanized nail plate
over the heart

275mm MINIMUM FOR
175x175 HARDWOOD
with heart centre

expected unsound
heart is 100x100

350mm MINIMUM FOR
100x100 HARDWOOD

expected unsound
heart is 112x112

350mm MINIMUM FOR
200x75 HARDWOOD

unsound heart is
minimum of 150x150

510mm MINIMUM FOR
150x150 HARDWOOD

Outdoor Structures Australia
Practical solutions that enhance community design projects
Old College Road, Gatton, Queensland, Australia
PO Box 517, Gatton, Queensland, Australia. 4343
Ph: (07) 5462 4255   Fax: (07) 5462 4077
Email: timber.tek@uq.net.au   Website: www.outdoorstructures.com.au

Date	CUTTING PATTERNS	Description
30/01/2003	FOR	
Drawn	PINE AND HARDWOOD	
J MILLARD		

Approved	Scale	Job No	Drawing No
E.M.S.	N.T.S.	OSA	CP1

Figure 6. Different size logs needed to cut different size timbers.

The heart (wood generally within 50 mm of the pith) of Australian hardwoods is less durable and softer than the outer heartwood. Under AS 2082-2000 heart was only permitted in structural timber when the size was at least 175x175 mm. (Designers should resist attempts by most suppliers to provide 150x150 mm with heart in, despite changes to AS2082 in 2007 – see Deadly Sin 5). Figure 6 shows the size of log needed to cut various sizes of sawn timber. It is obvious that large cross sections free of heart are very difficult to supply Because of the quality of the saw log presently available

Figure 7. Bollard with heart in centre has split

The 200x100 bollard I provided to my customers requires a relatively large log, which, in turn, makes the timber, cost comparatively expensive. If heart can be used, the log size decreases dramatically. 150 mm square with heart in can be cut from plantation thinning that are 225 mm diameter but, when free of heart, it requires a diameter of at least 510 mm High quality logs this size available for harvesting are scarce. As logs get larger they tend to have developed more natural features (a marketing term for defect) so the number of suitable logs is even less. In Australia, large quantities of timber are cut for landscaping which have no restriction on the amount of heart included. These are loosely called *sleepers (See Deadly Sin 4)*.

Some people use sleepers for landscaping bollards. Bollards made from low-grade timber can deteriorate quickly. The bollard in Figure 7, which attempts to copy our heart free product, was only three months old when the image was taken and already split.

I generally avoided using anything less than 175x175 mm with heart in the centre though there may be a small amount of heart on the edge of the 200x100 mm. Timber should be graded so that major defects are set in the ground.

Figure 8. Top of 200x200 bollard showing split.

Larger bollards, say 200x200 mm, are visually very effective but the heart causes major problems. The outside of the timber is shrinking while the inside stays the same size as there is no moisture loss. This causes the post to split down one side and across the top as shown in Figures 8 and 9.

The images in Figures 8 and 9 above are from a project OSA refused to supply as the specification was inadequate. We would have only supplied them with a metal cap and multiple expansion grooves down the length of the bollard. The client, as often happens, took the lower specification and price option and the bollards tore badly down the length and split the top. There are gaps so big that children can catch their fingers. OSA was then called on to supply the client with a metal cap seen in Figure 11, but the unsightly tear remains.

Figure 9. Side of 200x200 bollard showing split.

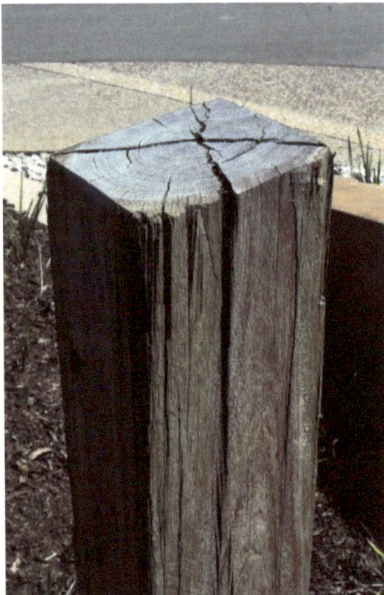

Figure 10. An expensive recycled post splitting badly

The problem of splitting is not avoided by using recycled timber. Large sizes are too big to season effectively and when the original timber is re-sawn they invariably behave just like a piece of new timber and are still likely to split, much to the frustration of the owner. We saw a case early in 2002 of recycled 200x200 mm turpentine which shrunk almost 10% in a few months.

The post in Figure 11 is 150x150 mm with the heart in the centre. Because the heart is much softer and less durable than the surrounding true wood, the centre decays as the image shows. A metal cap would protect this soft timber from decay and also restrains the top and helps minimise the splitting.

Figure 11. 150x150 with heart in is starting to degrade.

Figure 12. 200x200 post with cap.

The cap illustrated in Figure 12 is a standard OSA product. It is smaller than the post as it is designed to allow for a sawing tolerance of +9 mm or – 3 mm for sizes 200 mm and over[1] (despite what AS2082-2007 says). (Sizes under 200 mm have a tolerance of + or – 3 mm.

---

[1] As per AS2082-1979. The tolerance of + or – 2 mm of AS2082-2007 is wishful thinking.

Figures 7-11 should make one question why would you ever use heart centre for landscaping? When detailed properly it will age gracefully and is environmentally sound. This heart centre timber can be cut from regrowth and plantation timber, which should have considerable attraction to local government specifiers and environmentalists. Even though my living has been from native hardwoods, I have difficulty putting prime hardwood logs into landscaping. There are three points necessary for successfully using heart in hardwood bollards:

- The top must be capped
- A series of expansion grooves, (saw cut made up the full length of the bollard) are required. Multiple cuts allows the post to flex on an unobtrusive line rather than tear randomly down one side
- The timber must be one of a very limited range of species that have historically been proven to work. A blanket durability 1 or 2 specification is fraught with problems.

Figure 13., Post top prepared for cap.

All this is accommodated by simply purchasing a Pioneer Post developed by one of the licensees to OSA's IP!

Deadly Sin 4 - Use of Sleepers in Landscaping

Careful attention should be given when using the word "sleepers" in engineering and landscaping design as the designer's expectation seldom match what is received. This can lead to structural issues and aesthetic problems.

In Queensland, for over 100 years, when railway sleepers (or ties as they are called in some countries) were replaced they were simply stacked by the side of the line and burnt. While the sleepers had passed their use by date for their original purpose many were still sound enough to be used in structural landscaping applications such as retaining walls. It has been common practice for some time now for sleepers that have been withdrawn from service to make their way into the landscaping industry.

Figure 14. Landscape sleepers have no quality control.

Railway sleepers are produced from a limited range of species that have been proven to work well in fully weather exposed situations. They are not treated and the sapwood soon decays. In Queensland the standard size for a railway sleeper is 2150 mm long, 230 mm wide, and 115 or 150 mm thick and weigh approximately 70kg. Every sleeper was inspected before acceptance for compliance against a tight quality specification and annually thereafter over their service life of 20 years. They would have achieved a much longer life if they detailed correctly! They actually take more load cycles than concrete sleepers.

The quantity of used railway sleepers (and their size) did not meet the needs of the landscaping industry and soon sawmills started producing a timber product at about 50% the cost of the comparable size structural hardwood which they called *sleepers*. These were generally 200x50 mm, 200x75 mm and 200x100 mm and available in 2.4 m lengths. The only way that the timber could be produced so inexpensively was not to have any meaningful quality specifications. Invariably:

- Timber was cut with the heart (pith) fully in the centre or at the edge. Under AS2082, heart was not allowed in structural timber under 175x175 mm until a revision in 2007 (and then only for certain species). Included heart in smaller sizes results in timber that has no known structural value so cannot be used in structural design. The deterioration around the heart is dramatic as Figures 14 to 19 show.

- In some (most?) mills there was little selection of species as to suitability and little grading of natural defect. A general grading was *one reasonable face and edge*
- These "sleepers" contained very little sapwood yet were treated and stamped with the H4 or H5 brand. A practice that is only meaningful on hardwood which is durability class 1 in ground.

Unfortunately, these low grade, non structural products are being used in structural applications such as retaining walls where the specification is critical. They are also being used as non structural public landscaping but where long term appearance is required. I have seen footbridges designed by engineers with 200x50 mm sleepers as the only specification for decking and we have also seen bridges where this grade has been used! I have also seen drawings from landscape architects where the only timber specification is "sleepers".

Figure 15. Low quality timber used as retaining wall post.

Figure 16. Wall made from low quality timber

The sleeper wall in Figures 15 to 17 used timber of low quality which deteriorated quickly. One waler, the horizontal member in a retaining wall, has already been replaced. This retaining wall would not have been designed using this grade of timber. The sleepers would have been supplied on the basis of price and, not specification

The post in Figure 17 has not been supplied to an adequate durability specification, most likely compounded by setting the post in concrete – something you should not do with hardwood (see Deadly Sin 6). No fines concrete is acceptable though.

Figure 17. Post failing.

The bollard in Figure 18 is free of heart but has a very large unsound knot which is visually unacceptable in public landscaping. The bollard in Figure 19 has split in two because it was cut with the heart in. The nail plates on the tops of these bollards which are intended to restrain future degrade will, in time, be forced out of the end grain and endanger the public with their sharp corners. Both these bollards were specified as OSA products which are performance driven and replaced with sleepers on the basis of price.

Figure 18. Bollard with large knot.

As a footnote to Figures 18 and 19, the supplier boasted that "Ted does all the advertising and I get all the orders". If you are buying on price you are very unwise.

Figure 19. Nailplate attempting to hold bollard together

Deadly Sin 5 – 150x150 mm Hardwood in Landscaping

Figure 20. 150x150 with heart in supplied for bollards.

If specifying timber to get what you expect was not enough of a challenge, it has now become even harder. If you are not worried about appearance and performance of weather exposed timber don't read on. If this is of vital concern you will need to get your mind around something very complex. The 2007 revision to Australian Standard 2082 demands designers requiring high performance, appearance grade hardwood to carefully consider allowances for heart-in material.

The earlier standard only allowed boxed heart in sections greater than 175x175 mm in structural hardwood. This meant that a conforming 150x150 mm had to be supplied free of heart. The new standard, (clause 2.2.2. (e) (B) (ii)) now allows heart in many of the commonly available species from Queensland so long as it does not exceed one ninth of the cross sectional area for Structural Grade 2, i.e. for an F17 150x150 mm the heart, which can now be at the edge cannot exceed 28 mm in diameter.

Note: Specifying F17 appearance grade does not assist you in ensuring you receive timber free of included heart as it is not one of the exclusions for that grade.

What is heart? AS-NZS 4491 (Timber, Glossary of terms in timber related standards) defines it as "timber adjacent to or including the pith that is within 50 mm of the centre of the pith", i.e. a section 100 mm square boxed about the heart. That is simple and is in keeping with our experience and rules out any heart in a 150x150 mm. The problem is that in 2010, AS2082 redefines the meaning of "heart". In clause 1.4.4 it is now "The growth centre (pith) of the tree and/or timber adjacent to the growth centre of the tree that exhibits fungal attack, brittle heart and compression failure". Despite being a miller for 25 years and a qualified grader I do not know how to interpret that clause.

The note to the clause mentioned says "The allowance in item (ii) only relates to the primary structural properties of the timber. **For applications where appearance or other serviceability issues are important it may be appropriate to restrict inclusion of heart, pith and heart shakes**" (emphasis mine). That means the responsibility lies with the supplier if he/she knows the application and performance expectations as well as you the designer, to ensure material fit for use is received. In practical terms there is much more opportunity for unsuitable material to be supplied and it will be more difficult to shift responsibility to a producer who will simply say he was not made aware the higher expectations.

We recommend designers not specify structural 150x150 mm apart from a few feature pieces. We recommend that for structural timbers 150x100 mm be used in preference. Larger square bollards should be either 125x125 mm which can be supplied free of heart (but will need to be specified that way) or a minimum of 175x175 mm heart centre (better still use our Pioneer Post) with a metal cap. This is better use of a very limited resource and also will virtually eliminate the possibility of the substitution of an inappropriate use of heart in material and the awarding of the contract to "conforming" but unsuitable timber. The visual effect will be very similar to the required 150x150 mm. Where the client is adamant that 150x150 mm is required for a large quantity of bollards heart centre material must be accepted but with the addition of a cap and correctly detailed. Grading and species are still extremely important but lower performance must be accepted. More on detailing these posts can be found in our guide, Grading Hardwood (Understanding AS2082).

You can talk to us about your landscaping needs and now be even more cautious of the lowest tender.

Deadly Sin 6 – Setting Hardwood Posts in Concrete

Figure 21. Pole in concrete decayed at ground line. Image courtesy of Timber Queensland

It is a very common practice to set hardwood posts in concrete due to its simplicity. It could almost be classed as universal practice.

OSA became aware of problems associated with mixing hardwood and concrete many years ago when it was supplying powerpoles. At a conference the then Officer in Charge, of Wood Chemistry & Preservation of the Queensland Department of Forestry referred to this decay as "Victa[2] disease". This was because the decay was aggravated by situations such as a domestic footpath where there was frequent watering and the addition of fertilizer. It is a situation many landscaping projects would experience. As the timber shrinks a gap develops between the post and the concrete so moisture is trapped while fertilizer promotes decay organisms. The problem is not solved by only specifying (and hopefully receiving) Durability 1 In-ground timber. I have seen an iron bark pole rot off at ground level within 14 years.

For our landscaping products we recommend backfilling with any one of these three options:

- Natural earth if suitable
- Fine crushed rock
- No fines concrete

OSA's recommendation for no fines concrete follows that of Timber Queensland in its *Technical Data Sheet No. 9 Timber Retaining Walls for Residential Applications* where it says:

No fines concrete shall be 10mm maximum aggregate size, 450 kg cement per m³ and a water cement ratio of 0.55. The concrete shall be Readymixed or hand mixed manufactured to the requirements of AS 1379. For no fines concrete the concrete shall be well agitated immediately before placing to ensure a complete coating of the aggregate. The concrete shall be discharged directly into the holes and tamped without delay. All concrete shall be placed within one hour of batching. The no fines concrete shall not be reworked as this destroys the bond.

It further states (which is more important for structural applications)

---

[2] For overseas readers, a Victa is a very popular lawn mower in Australia.

For no fines concrete top the last 100 mm with clay to prevent surface infiltration into the backfill.

For large free standing In-ground timber structures such as totems the advice of a specialist timber engineer should be sought. Alternatively members should contact Timber Queensland for advice.

At this stage we are not aware of decay problems related to correctly treated pine and concrete.

Figure 22. Taxi hit by falling pole. Image courtesy of Timber Queensland

Deadly Sin 7 – Relying on AS5604 for Determining Durability

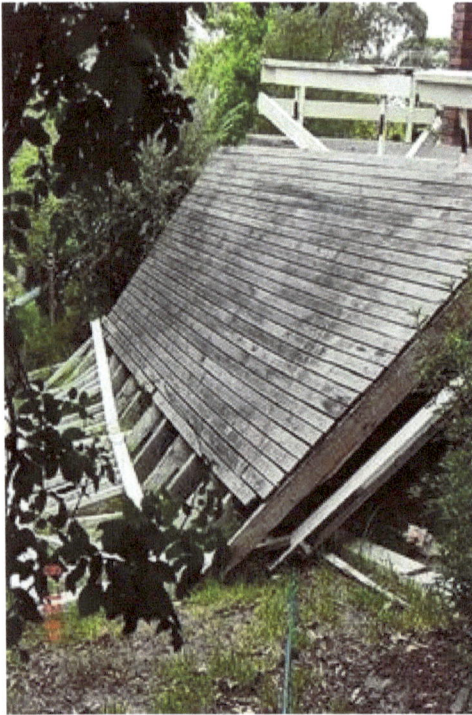

Figure 23. Incorrect selection of timber durability can lead to structural failure. Image from Archicentre press release.

AS5604 Timber – natural durability ratings is being applied inappropriately and leading to premature failure of weather exposed structures and decking. How often do you see an industry warn about one of its own related Australian Standards? The following, a Timber Queensland update to their Technical Bulletin of June 2004 is such a warning, where the problem is stated very clearly.

"Timber Queensland still has concerns relating to the interpretation and application of **Above-ground** durability ratings now given for species listed in AS 5604.

In some quarters, the new above ground durability ratings given in this standard are being used to justify permanent, long term, above ground weather exposed applications (H3) for species where previously these species (based upon In-ground ratings) were not considered appropriate for long term application.

AS 5604 has a table that links the In-ground and above ground durability rating of species to a probable life expectancy as shown below.

Class	Probable In-ground life expectancy (years)	Probable Above-ground life expectancy (years)
1	Greater than 25	Greater than 40
2	15 to 25	15 to 40
3	5 to 15	7 to 15
4	0 to 5	0 to 7
Table 1 - Natural durability - probable life expectancy (see below).		

The ratings in this table are based on expert opinions and the performance of the following test specimens:
- In-ground: 50 x 50 mm test specimens at five sites around Australia.
- Above-ground: 35 x 35 mm test specimens at eleven sites around Australia.

As further reliable evidence becomes available, these ratings may require amending. The heartwood of an individual piece of timber may vary from the species' nominated classification. "Above-ground" conditions equate to "outside Above-ground" subject to periodic moderate wetting when ventilation and drainage are adequate.

As can be seen from this table, the In-ground life expectancies for each class are the same as they have always been and, the historical expectation was that species with an **In-ground rating** of Class 1 or 2 would have above ground life expectancies of around 40 years plus which when coupled with appropriate maintenance etc, satisfies the implicit performance expectations of our current building regulations.

Within AS 5604, as can be seen from the following table, many species that are rated Class 2 or better In-ground are rated Class 1 above ground and species rated Class 3 In-ground are rated Class 2 above ground, whilst other species ratings do not change.

Species	Heartwood - In Ground Durability Class	Heartwood - Above Ground Durability Class
Ash, silvertop	3	2
Blackbutt	2	1
Gum, blue, Sydney	3	2
Gum rose	3	2
Gum, spotted	2	1
Ironbark	1	1
Jarrah	2	2
Kapur	3	2
Kwila	3	1
Stringybark, brown	3	2
Table 2. In ground and above ground durability comparisons.		

It is obvious from the above table that is extracted from AS 5604 and the Table above it, that just because species are now rated Class 2 above ground, does not mean that they will now perform any better than they have historically e.g. rose gum."

As specifiers and users of timber, to avoid the difficulties with AS5604, Outdoor Structures encourages you to use our current recommendations together with Timber Queensland's recently updated Technical Data Sheets. You should also be updating your libraries with Construction Timbers in Queensland' which is available free of charge over the internet or can be purchased as a hard copy from the Queensland Government bookstore.

Deadly Sin 8 – Using White Cypress Externally

Figure 24. Cypress logs in a mill yard.

White cypress was classed as a Durability 1 In-ground species (the highest) but recent codes have downgraded it to Durability 2 In-ground while still remaining and Above Ground 1.

When a technical publication refers to the natural durability of a species it refers to the heartwood, otherwise known as the truewood. This is the timber directly behind the sapwood. Sapwood in cypress is easily distinguished as the band of lighter coloured timber at the outside of the log. The heart (or pith) and heartwood are much darker. No sapwood is durable, irrespective of the species whether it is ironbark (In-ground Durability 1) or radiata pine (In-ground Durability 4). All sapwood is classed as In Ground or Above Ground Durability 4 depending on the application.

Sapwood of many species can be made durable by treatment. Cypress, however, is classed as a *refractory* species because it does not treat well with waterborne preservatives such as CCA, Tanalith E and ACQ. This means that, in Queensland, when the Timber Utilisation and Marketing Act was in place is was illegal to sell cypress with a claim that it preserved with any of these preservatives. Most likely, it will not comply with the specified penetration and retention for the species/hazard class combination. Unfortunately for Victoria and other states that do not have a Timber Utilisation and Marketing Act, "anything can go" and quite frequently does. Queensland is now in their company.

Unlike hardwood, the heart (this is different to heartwood) or pith of the cypress log is structural, This allows small members such as 100x100 mm to be cut, boxed around the pith giving a member without sapwood. The small nature of most logs limit the member size that can be achieved this way. Rectangular members are cut to give the maximum recovery from the log and so these can contain a large amount of sapwood. Is it possible to order the timber free of sapwood? My contacts in the industry would not even accept orders for even ex 100x25 mm product free of sapwood though I understand that some will.

Apart from the exception of smaller size boxed heart given above, Cypress should not be considered suitable for structural purposes for **fully weather exposed** external use such as boardwalks and decking where a long trouble free life is required. Appropriate uses for cypress are as covered framing where its termite resistance is required or as attractive internal flooring. Some are reporting reasonable service as decking under a roof.

There has been success with LOSP treatment on boards up to 25 mm thick. Unfortunately in 2013 the company selling these boards ceased operation and at the time of writing the product is not available. These boards are too thin for commercial decks.

Conclusion

You have read through my eight pet hates in timber design. If you were to make up your own list I expect that some of these might be included and you would have others included as your life experience and the industry segment you are involved will have been different to mine.

When you look at these eight problems and the solution to them, there is nothing illogical or unreasonable in this, it all makes sense and it is all very simple. If you have a problem area of design, supply or construction that you keep encountering please share it with me. The whole industry can learn from it and avoid it in future.

www.ingramcontent.com/pod-product-compliance
Lightning Source LLC
Chambersburg PA
CBHW060807270336
41927CD00002B/75